D1415686

I publish, therefore I am.
Cable

# Cable on Academe

== Cartoons by Carole Cable ==

University of Texas Press, Austin

For T.C.




Printed in the United States of America
First edition, 1994



♾ The paper used in this publication meets the minimum requirements of
American National Standard for Information Sciences—Permanence of Paper
for Printed Library Materials, ANSI Z39.48-1984.

*Library of Congress Cataloging-in-Publication Data*

Cable, Carole.
Cable on academe / cartoons by Carole Cable. — 1st ed.
p. cm.
ISBN 0-292-71170-0 (pbk. : acid-free paper)
1. Education—Caricatures and cartoons. 2. American wit and humor, Pictorial.
I. Title.
NC1429.C13A4 1994
741.5'973—dc20 93-48668

# Cable on Academe

Of the 124 cartoons in *Cable on Academe*, 115 originally appeared in *The Chronicle of Higher Education*; 8 in *The Chronicle of Philanthropy*; and 1 in the *Graduate Gazette* of The University of Texas at Austin.

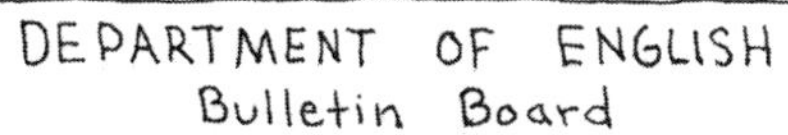
DEPARTMENT OF ENGLISH
Bulletin Board

Cable

SUGGESTIONS

DIATRIBES

DISCOURSES

*"The fact that his textbook sold 80,000 copies last year, I'm assuming, should not be held against him."*

*"The first year of the college's Five-Year Plan will be devoted to reading it."*

HISTORY BUILDING

CAMPUS DIRECTORY

POND

○ Needs new plumbing
□ Needs new roof
△ Needs elevator
▭ Needs new windows

cable

*"Before we adjourn, let's decide on the agenda, so we can put something in the minutes."*

*"Touch of ennui."*

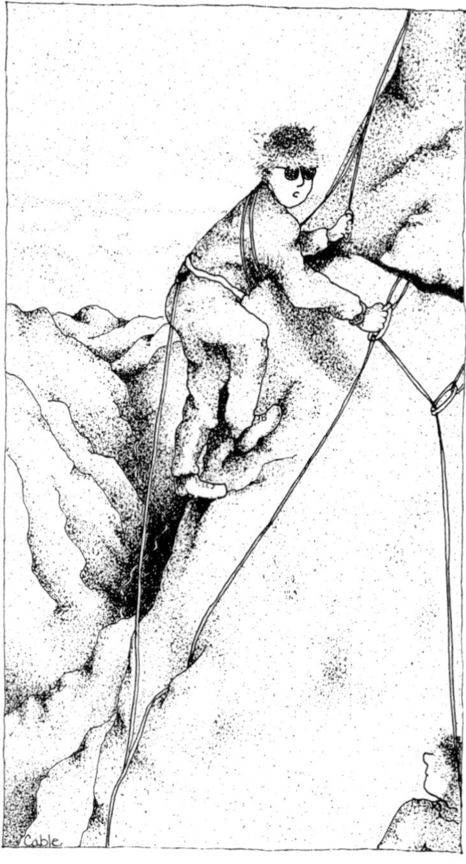


*"What I hate most about this is the annual report."*

*"Yes, but just suppose Yale did mount a takeover bid for Harvard!"*

*"His appearance on the Phil Donahue Show is not, I'm afraid, sufficient cause to deny tenure."*

*"I can assure the board that our annual tuition increases have been well below our annual rate of grade inflation."*

*"Comin' 'round the bend—big, really big subcommittee."*

COLLEGE
ESTABLISHED 1839
BESIEGED 1967-1972
IGNORED 1973-1986
SUED 1987
cable

NOTICE
FACULTY MEETING TODAY 4:00
Haven't had a quorum in 20 years. This might be the day.
Cable

*"A real tour de force—he went from Aristotelian logic to Neo-Cartesian reality to 'downsizing' in less than ten minutes."*

Each new member of this committee brings to it a lifetime of hopes, desires, dreams fulfilled and unfulfilled, some regrets, a multitude of aspirations, a wealth of academic and professional accomplishments, and a sense of intellectual rigor charged with a panoply of talent that guarantees even greater success as we endeavor to make our world what it should and must be ....
This *is* the Parking and Traffic Committee?
Cable

UNIVERSITY
ROTC LIBRARY
Rotate material to assume horizontal position with the end parallel to rectangular opening. Initiate an insertion into opening. Move material forward. Release. Repeat as necessary.
cable

ORIGIN OF THE SABBATICAL.

*"Needs some revision."*

*"Old post-structuralists never die, Thurston; they just become deans."*

# MID-LIFE CRISIS: ACADEMIC VERSION

*"Today Miami sealed its trade of two Chaucerians and a dean for a Nobel Prize winner out of Stanford, now of Chicago. And in an unexpected move, Houston traded a third-year sociologist to Michigan for a first-round pick at MLA."*

THE ACADEMIC LECTURE CIRCUIT

Cable

*"On that ridge there—big scouting party from the MacArthur Foundation."*

cable

*"It's not the résumé of a committee-kind-of-guy."*

CABLE

*"The academic conference will remain intellectually and professionally viable only so long as there are large hotels with slow elevators."*

# A SURE THING

*"It's an offer for $20,000 more <u>and</u> a designated parking space."*

THIS SPACE
FOR
RENT
CALL 5625427
NO
SMOKING
YOUR DRIVER:
ED SIMS
A. B. SWARTHMORE
PH.D. COLUMBIA
WRITE P.O. BOX 236
FOR COMPLETE
VITA
Cable

Cable

*"I've decided to lip sync my next MLA paper."*

*"Let me emphasize. This is a re-creation of a paper given in Maui in '84 and Boca Raton in '87."*

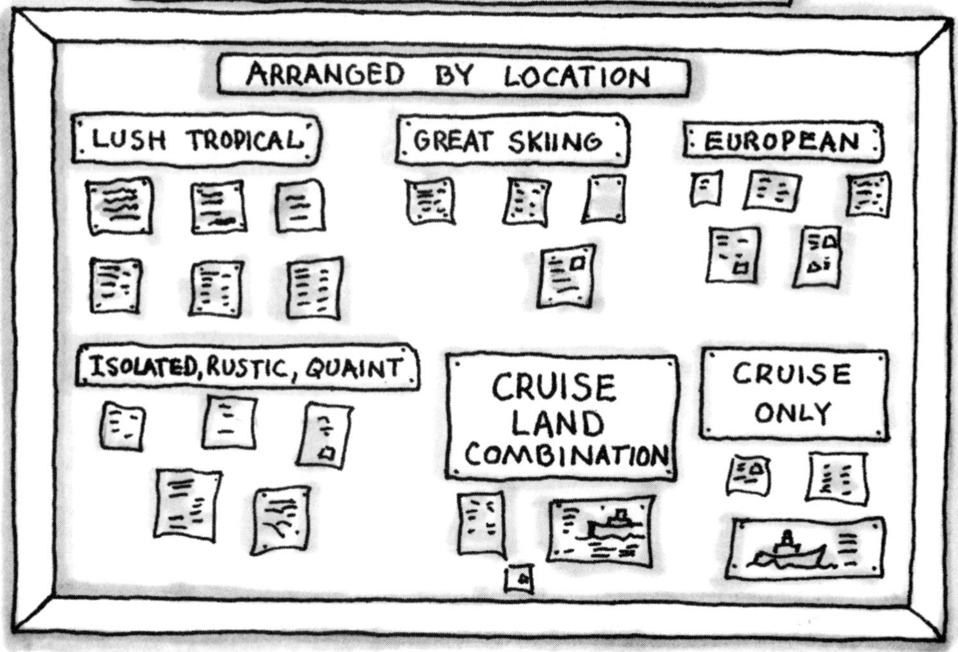
CONFERENCES, SYMPOSIA
ARRANGED BY LOCATION
LUSH TROPICAL
GREAT SKIING
EUROPEAN
ISOLATED, RUSTIC, QUAINT
CRUISE LAND COMBINATION
CRUISE ONLY
cable

*"No, really, I am pleased that you called me on your cellular phone from your BMW to tell me your paper will be late."*

*"I loved those complex, uninhibited, sometimes erotic, tales with their ample dose of mystery and mayhem. Now they just say 'faulty disk' when they turn in a late paper."*

T. P.
"No Prerequisite"
SIMS
cable

*"Let me see if I've got this. You're going to get a second opinion and check back with me later?"*

T. D. SIMSON
PROFESSOR
POPULAR CULTURE

LET'S RAP
M, F 1-2

CABLE

*"Timothy Leary? I quoted him once as an undergraduate, but I never read him."*

*"I know the final exam comes at a really bad time. Summer school comes at a really bad time."*

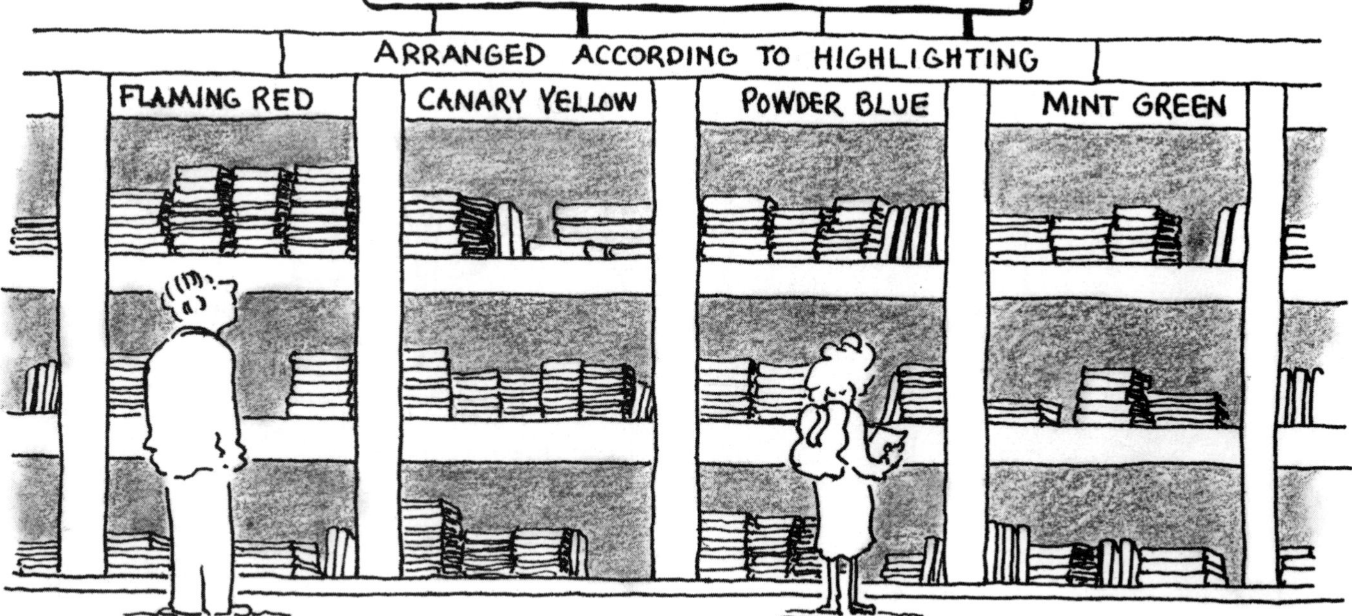
USED TEXTBOOKS
ARRANGED ACCORDING TO HIGHLIGHTING
FLAMING RED
CANARY YELLOW
POWDER BLUE
MINT GREEN
cable

*"Really strange fellow. I hear he grades his own exams."*

REGISTRATION

INTRODUCTORY COURSES

| COURSE | INSTRUCTOR | TIME | ODDS ON GETTING IN |
|---|---|---|---|
| ART 103 | SIMS | M,W,F 1:00 | 2-1 |
| BIOLOGY 101 | A. SMITH | T,T 10:30 | 12-1 |
| DRAMA 106 | BRONOUSKI | T,T 9:00 | 8-1 |
| ENGLISH 108 | ADAMS | M,W,F 10:00 | 16-1 |
| FRENCH 113 | MALONEY | M,W,F 12:00 | 10-1 |
| GEOLOGY 110 | STOTT | M,W,F 2:30 | 12-1 |
| ITALIAN 102 | FIORRUCCI | T,T, 9:30 | even |
| MARKETING 104 | CONRAD | T,T 1:30 | 32-1 |
| PSYCHOLOGY 105 | WILLIAMS | M,W,F 3:00 | 16-1 |
| RUSSIAN 102 | JAMESON | M,W,F 8:30 | 3-2 |
| THEATER 104 | TIMS | T,T 2:00 | 7-1 |

INTERNSHIPS
Paying Interesting
Non-Paying Interesting
Neither
Cable

Prof. E. S. James, Inc.
Dept. of Finance
Cable

REGISTRATION
FRESHMAN ENGLISH
ENG 301 SEC 8 MWF 8:00 - 9:00
* ENG 301 SEC 3 MWF 11:00 - 12:00
ENG 301 SEC 2 TTH 10:00 - 11:30
ENG 301 SEC 6 TTH 12:00 - 1:30
ENG 301 SEC 1 MWF 9:00 - 10:00
* ENG 301 SEC 5 TTH 9:00 - 10:30
ENG 301 SEC 4 MWF 2:00 - 3:00
ENG 301 SEC 9 MWF 3:00 - 4:00
ENG 301 SEC 7 TTH 11:00 - 12:30
ENG 301 SEC 10 MWF 1:00 - 2:00
* HONORS SECTION. MUST BE ABLE TO READ AND WRITE.

cable

*"I'm pleased, Mr. Fenton, that Willa Cather and Herman Melville made your short list."*

QUIET PLEASE
Cable

NEXT ON GERALDO —
FRESHMEN WHO READ.
CABLE

*"Now, what's this about the greenhouse effect impeding the progress of your dissertation?"*

*"The graduate students thought it multiculturally significant that you added cilantro to the onion dip."*

Prof. T.P. Sims
2nd. ed., rev.
Cable

T.C. JENKINS
STATISTICIAN
24 HOURS A DAY
7 DAYS A WEEK
52 WEEKS A YEAR
Cable

*"I'm talking major stress. Last night I dreamed Barbara Bush called and asked to audit my Virginia Woolf seminar."*

*"My sophomore class informed me today that 'condom' can also be a verb."*

COURSES OFFERED NEXT SEMESTER

CABLE

*"A real lech. I hear he's teaching the Virginia Woolf seminar as part of his rehabilitation."*

DEPARTMENT OF ENGLISH

Cable

*"I too revere Hawthorne, Mr. Fenton, but wouldn't characterize him as 'Peter Greenawayish.'"*

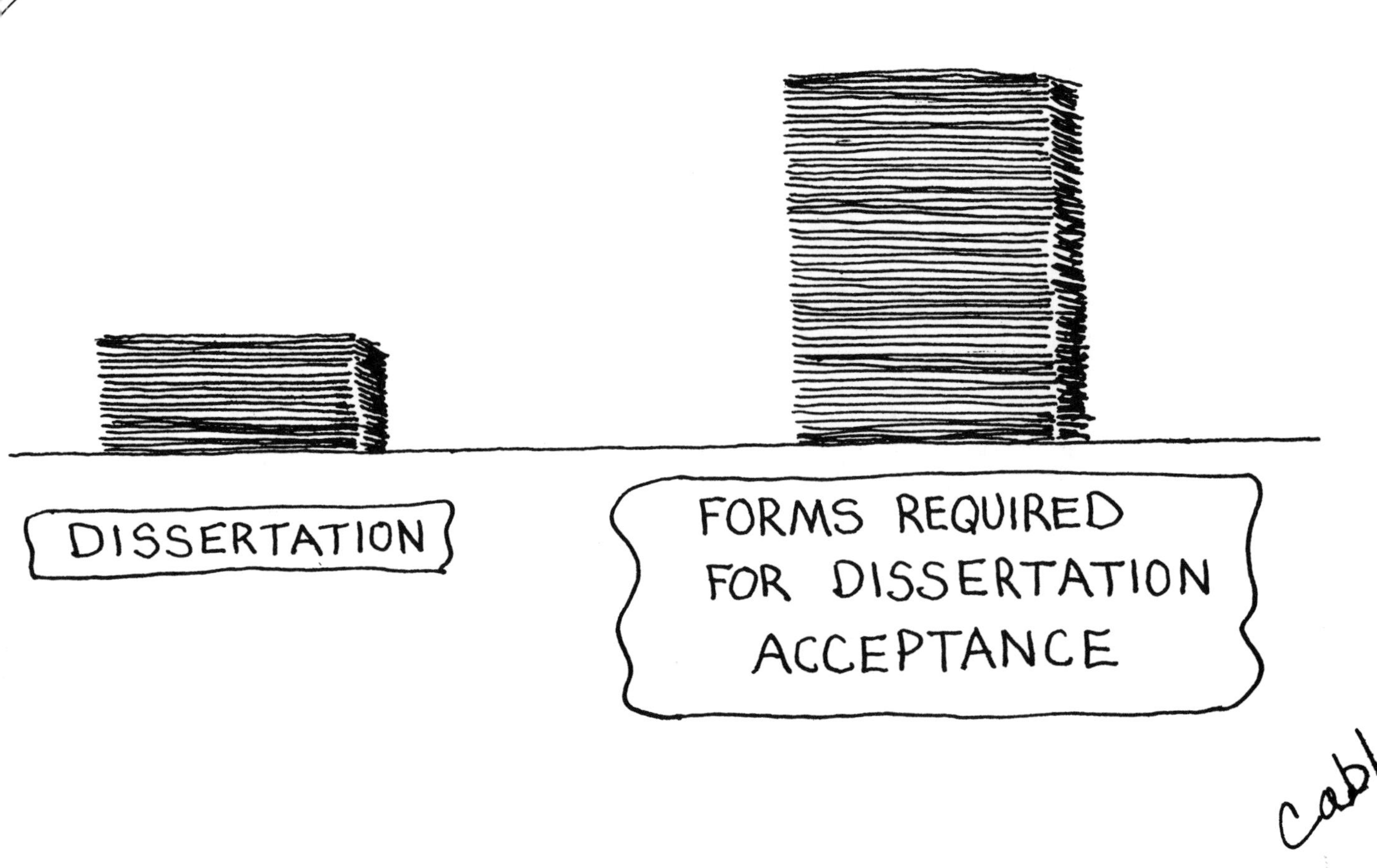
DISSERTATION
FORMS REQUIRED FOR DISSERTATION ACCEPTANCE
cable

*"I read that Camille Paglia was writing the preface to Madonna's new book . . . or was it the other way around?"*

SALE
GENERAL NON-FICTION BOOKS
NON-FICTION BOOKS WITH "SEMIOTICS" IN TITLE
Cable

*"You realize what this means. Ours will be the first-ever sociology series to have a monograph on Murphy Brown."*

*"No, really, I think it's wonderful that your oeuvre is biodegradable."*

*"An earlier version of this novel appeared two years ago as a manicotti recipe on the Internet."*

*"Right. I won't say, 'So this is the house the freshman textbook built.'"*

*"I'm writing a short story about our relationship. It's set in a wagon going west in 1849 and includes three chickens, a goat, and an old codger who spouts double entendres. You're one of the chickens."*

*"I've joined a men's support group, mind you, only to get me through the proofing."*

*"Really? My dissertation is also on Foucault and Mickey Rourke."*

*"I like it. It says 'tenured, but still publishing.'"*

DEPARTMENTAL LOUNGE
Thank you for not talking about your next book.
COFFEE
10¢
Cable

CABLE

*"If we published many books like this, Professor Haskens, we'd perish."*

*"J. Austen up on news of projected collected letters; Dickens stable as usual; Milton down due to recent negative comments; Pre-Raphaelites up on reports of joint venture with Bloomsbury Group; and Shakespeare down dramatically due to inventory buildup."*

*"Enough about my oeuvre. What about yours?"*

Cable

FLAVORS

TOPPINGS

Cable

*"Double sprinkles. Today's Times called my book 'seminal.'"*

*"Hemingway wrote two books there. That was, however, pre-Hilton."*

*"It'll be out next week and followed shortly thereafter by paperback, software, and puppet versions."*

*"Hardback, paper, audio, or 100-percent-cotton-T-shirt edition?"*

*"Normally we don't set up tours for authors of calculus texts."*

*"His persona is still in the rewrite stage. He's going to call me when he's renumbered the pages."*

CABLE

*"No part of this publication may be reproduced without a lot of trouble."*

*"I realize you're impressed with my collection of feminist essays. Just don't call it 'seminal.'"*

*"We have become very close, Ellen. We've shared a lot of good times. But, no, I can't help you index your new book."*

Cable

*"In lieu of a second book, I'm doing a haiku."*

*"It's too sordid and disgusting for me to talk about, especially now that it's developing into a short story."*

*"What you need is a grant to give you some free time to write a really first-rate grant proposal."*

*"If I had a grant, I'd eat out."*

*"Agreed. We fund all proposals with three appendices or less."*

*". . . brought to you by a grant from Mobil."*

Didn't get my grant
Lemonade $450.00
Cable

*"If you get a grant, but I don't; or if I get a grant, but you don't; or if we both get a grant; or if neither of us gets a grant, let's get married."*

*"There isn't a foundation, Mr. Jenkins, that specifically supports projects by middle-aged white men."*

*"Let me see if I've got this. You want a remote mountain cabin with fireplace, no phone, for two weeks so you can write a grant proposal?"*

*"I wish to thank the Guggenheim Foundation, the National Endowment for the Humanities, and the American Council of Learned Societies for all rejecting my grant proposals and forcing me to write this gothic science fiction sex-fantasy mystery novel that has brought me a seven-figure hardback advance."*

*"He was wild and crazy. I was wild and crazy. Then our grants ran out."*

"LET'S TRY COMMUNICATING IN MORSE CODE," HE TAPPED.

*"It's our daughter calling from Wesleyan. She would like to ask us a few questions about the Sixties."*

"It's happened to all of us. No matter how sensitive, how modern you are. But the fact that she told you you made a sexist remark is, I feel, a positive sign."

*"Anglo-Saxon England, if I may be so bold to suggest, is not electronically friendly."*

*"According to my calculations, the average scientific article has a half-life of three minutes."*

CABLE

TODAY'S ODDS
Makes totally black copies 3-1
Makes copies with wavy black lines 4-1
Misfeeds 2-1
Gives no change 3-1
Gives double change 8-1
Mystery light appears and 2 or more of the above occur 5-1
COPIES 20¢
Cable

*"Once I too was flappable."*

*"OK, but just suppose Thoreau had used E-mail."*

ACCESSING
LUNCH
BACK SOON
Cable

*"Could you be more specific than 'Let's co-mingle our books?'"*

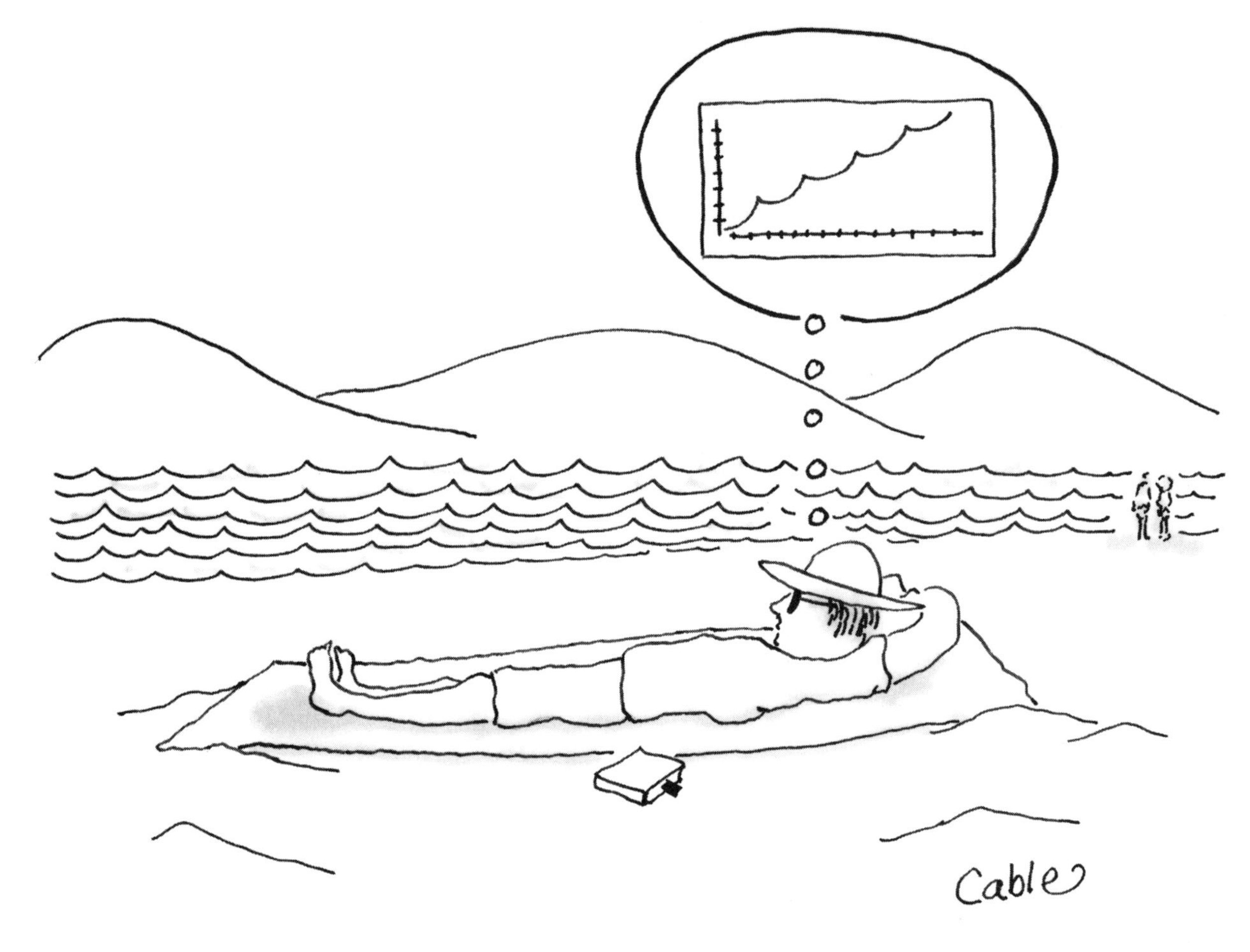
Cable

*"It says, 'This had been done before, but never with such bravado.'"*

NO POSTSTRUCTURALISTS
NEXT
72 MILES
Cable

# FETTUCCINE ALFREDO*:

## THE FOOTNOTES

cable

---

*This dinner is made possible in part through assistance from Tom who did the shopping and cleaned up.

[1] For a slight variation on the methodology used in this work, see my <u>Linguini with Canned Tomato Sauce</u> (1984– Tuesdays and Thursdays– ).

[2] I am indebted to my distinguished colleague, Prof. L. Sietzin, History Department, for providing me with critical information concerning the location of dried wild mushrooms. The raspberry vinaigrette dressing owes much to research conducted during a Fulbright year in Grenoble, 1981.

[3] (Orvieto: 1983)

[4] See my forthcoming <u>Puff Pastry</u> for my most indepth usage of cream to date.

[5] Placemat (with view of English village, ca. 1780/rpt. Victoria & Albert Museum Shop, 1985) while contextually ambiguous, did not require ironing.

WARNING
The following play, written by
a 16th century British upper
middle class white male
may be offensive or
irrelevant to some
audiences. Viewer
discretion advised.

Cable

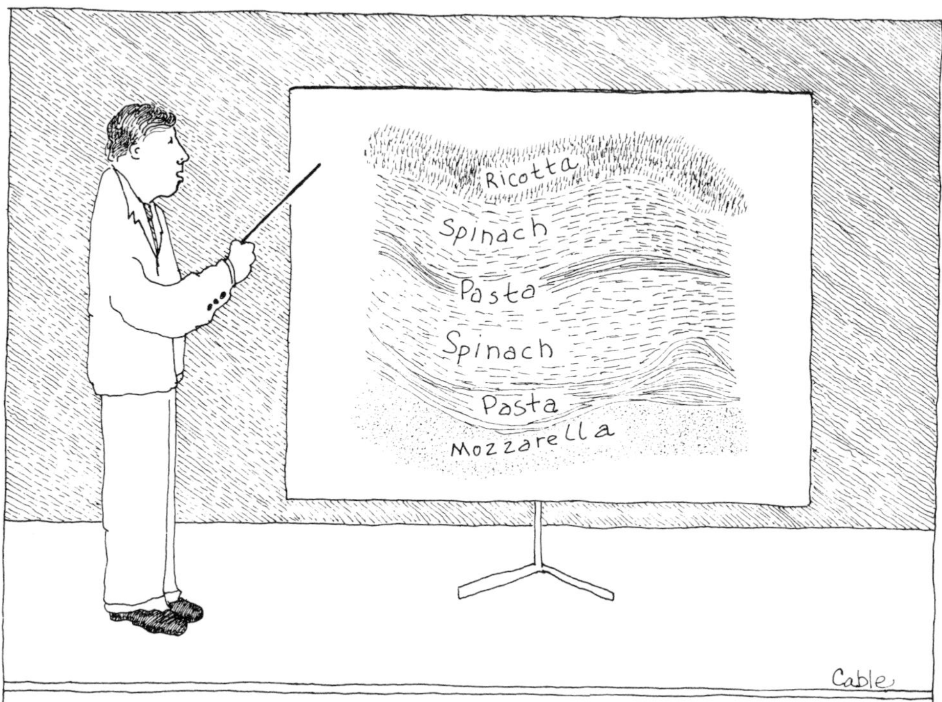


HIS DINOSAUR EXTINCTION THEORY WAS BASED ON THE VEGETABLE LASAGNA PARADIGM.

Cable

*"First thing next week we'll phase out our derivative late East Anglian naturalistic style and retool for an aggressively tactile, early Proto-Rheinish geometric."*

*"It's a lonely, dirty business, but," she sighed, "someone's got to look for subtexts."*

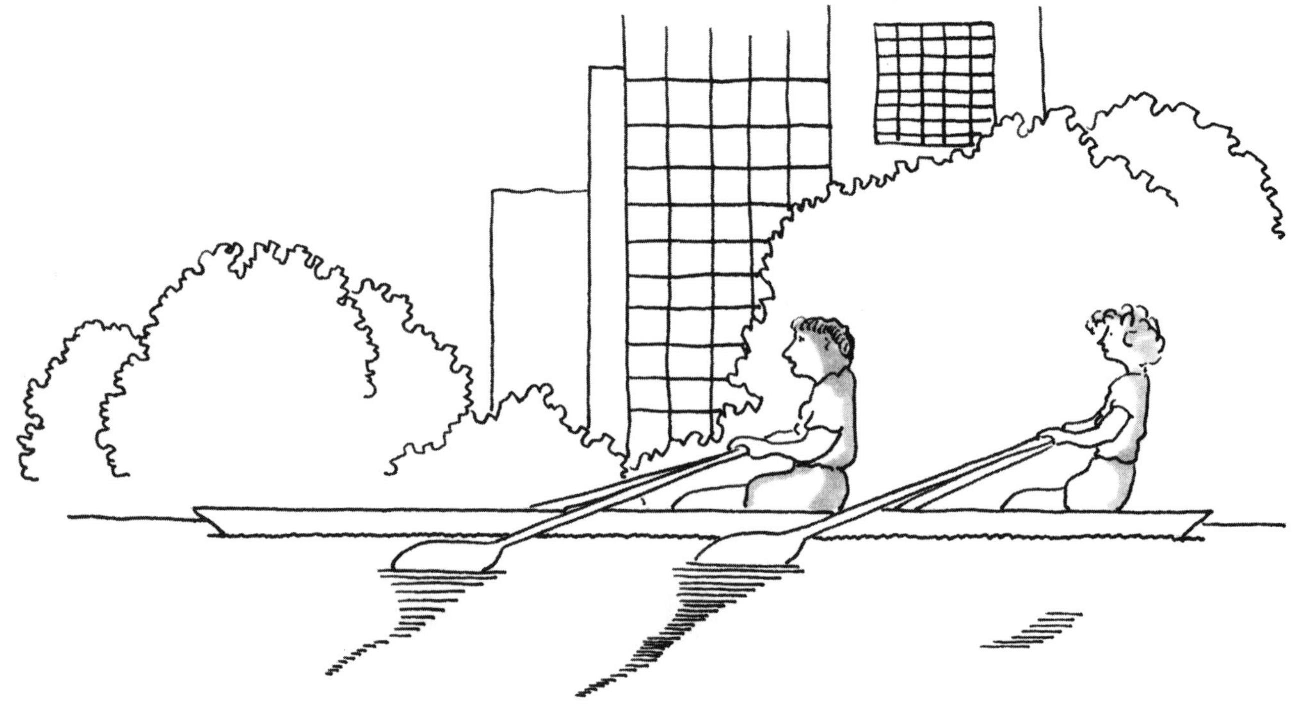


*"Emily, I can't row and discuss Umberto Eco at the same time."*

*"Don't quote me. Out of context it might sound a bit Camille Pagliaish."*

*"It has been noted that a discussion of the early novels of Edith Wharton is on Channel 2."*

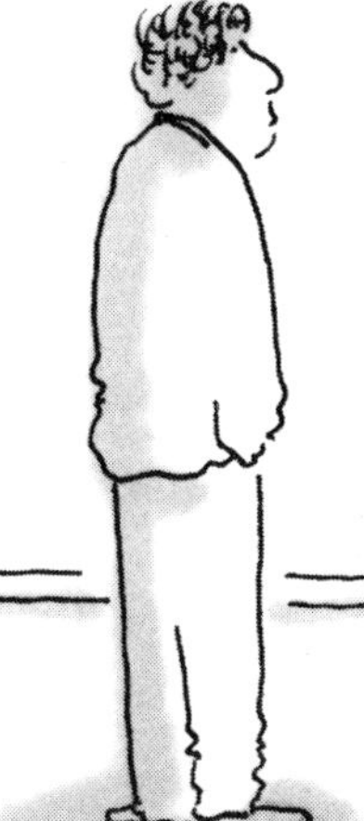
MUSEUM
GUIDE
Complex juxtapositions 3
Fluid articulations 2
Lucid manipulations 1
Powerful discourses 4
Vibrant archetypes 5
Cable

*"Hard to believe this is the same guy who turned in a 50-page annual report."*

T. P. "Messes with Paradigms" Sims

*"Soon you will subtextually relate to a tall, dark, and referentially hyperbolic postmodernist."*

*"Quantum mechanics, Harrison, is 100% multicultural."*

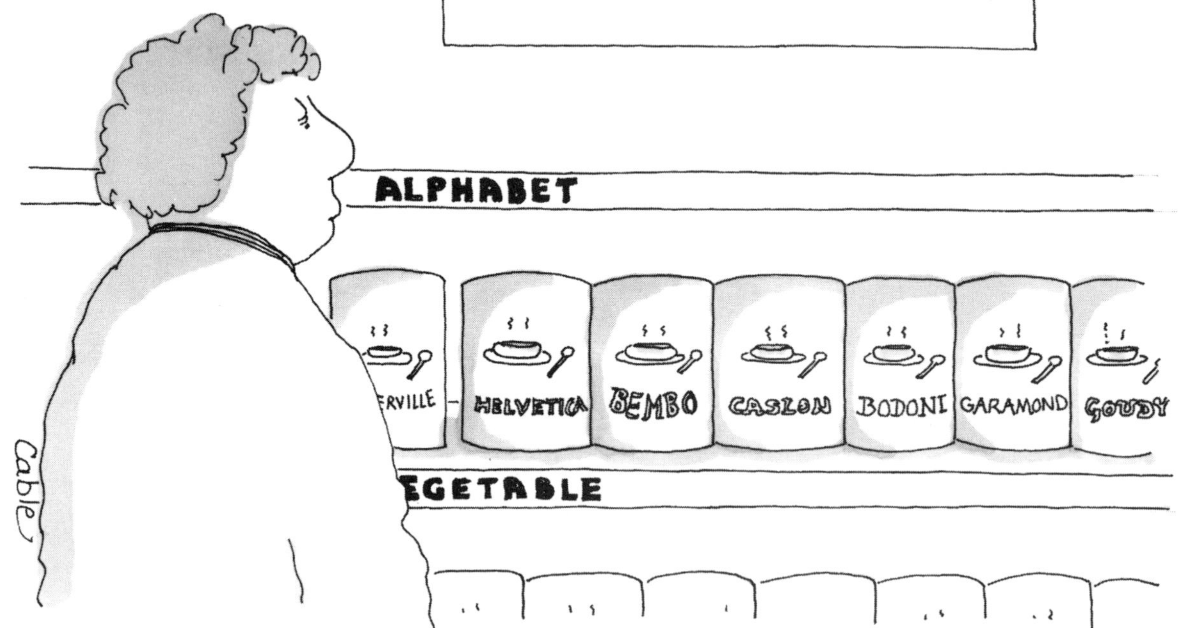
GOURMET SOUPS
ALPHABET
ERVILLE
HELVETICA
BEMBO
CASLON
BODONI
GARAMOND
GOUDY
EGETABLE
Cable

*"Neo-lasagna, post-moussaka, or late moo goo gai pan?"*

*"My pizza coupons."*

*"I may not know much about art, but I know how to write about it."*

Carole Cable's cartoons have appeared regularly in *The Chronicle of Higher Education* since 1987. They have also appeared in other publications, including *Art Papers*, *Audubon*, *Chicago*, *Datamation*, *The Medical Aspects of Human Sexuality*, *Natural History*, *Science*, and *The Wine Spectator*. She lives in Austin, Texas.